Studies of Continuity

Studies of Continuity

CIARAN PERKS

THE CHOIR PRESS

First published in the United Kingdom in 2021 by
The Choir Press

ISBN 978-1-78963-218-7

Contents

Hereditary and Feudal, Part One: Hereditary: Will Steam or Smoke Rise?

To inform
a character
of fourth-law
projection,
to alter
a Western
caricature's injection.

And I spoke–
I spoke about
'thirty-nine,
brink o',
know it well,
before what
finds now.
I spoke–
I said,

"Hey, Eastern Navy!
Have you got somethin' for me?"
And they said,
"Hey, Western Crew-Man!
Get out'a our league!"
And I spoke–
I said,
"Hey, Eastern Navy!
Your vessel,
largely particular,
follow more, 'berg
attraction,
fairest enemy."

And they swam,
they swam–
they did–
they swam,
passing borders,
but their
chimney of closed eyes . . .
Will steam or smoke rise?

To tell the stone
of commanding, commands,
the stone forms
the pointing of
six o'clock hands.

And a year later, I
stayed,
eastern-blue waves,
their waves
I say,
their ways,
I said,
"Hey, Eastern Corporal!
You got somethin' for me?"
And he said,
"Hey, Western Crew-Man!
Do yah walk boards, or
walk free?"

And I stopped–
I mumbled–
I stopped
and ran,
like their warnings
of attacking
my own foreign
land.

And they swam–
and they swam
further,
they did,
passing designation, wise–
and I asked his watching–
I asked,
"Will steam or smoke rise?"

Weary and drawn-out
and done,
December 'forty-one,
I slipped on my boots–
I asked,
"Hey, Eastern Fleet!
My hat over-sea,
you got somethin' for me?"

They opened their
bottles, bottom-chimney steam,
they screamed,
"We got diamonds and pearls
yet to gleam!"

And yet,
I saw last,
my hat over-sea,
the leaking,
bloody chimney.
I asked,
I begged–
I asked and
I watched their
dirty lies,
I said,
"Partner,
would yah tell me?
Will steam or smoke rise?"

Hereditary and Feudal, Part Two: Feudal: Oh, Does Smoke Rise!

To direct
a painting
from feudal hesitation,
the ignition,
a war invitation.

I prepared–
I knew,
I prepared,
I spoke,
"Hey, Eastern Territory!
You got somethin' new?"
They spread and they
choked,
"Hey, Western Crew-Man!
We rained only once,
you are wanted–
your country needs you!"

And I spoke–
"Is this real?
Is this true?"
And rubbing my
less-blind eyes,
I whispered,
"Hey, man . . .
Will steam or smoke rise?"

Chilly,
mid-winter,
January 'forty-five,
I directed a fleet,
preparing their
minds and behinds.

I looked–
and I asked those
once more,
"Hey, Eastern People!
You got somethin' new?"
They stuttered,
they applauded–
in shells they said,
"Hey, Western Crew-Man,
you want somethin' new?
We're afraid 'forty-one
'twas all we could do."

Inside I jolted–
electrical voltage,
I saw two calamities
of iris spies,
I asked no more
after,
no compromise–
"Will steam or smoke rise?"

Summer left me
hotter
than the palms of Florida,
I'll and I've–
I told them,
in August 'forty-five.

And I spoke–
I did,
I spoke about
this new time,
brink o',
know it well,
before what
finds now.

I spoke–
I said,
"Hey, East-Men,
I got somethin' for you!"
They, surprised,
they, impressed,
they talked,
they stressed,
"Hey, Western Crew-Man,
we say,
you're comin' for who?"

I spoke in the plains,
the wings, the plane,
I let go emotional artillery,
distilled successfully.
Orbs of white,
they ruined all light,
they looked from schools,
from hospices, bell-towers,
cold-showers, flowers,
mails, trails, boating-whales,
hump-back frost-biting–
they saw a falling lady,
her sweet demise,
in the clouds
of you-know-what,
I sighed,
"Oh, does smoke rise!"

The Philosophy of Modesty

Given to all by The Perception Administration/subsidiary organisations of The Perception Administration.

You may have received this statement through any means we have felt appropriate. It is a statement of dire importance. Please handle it with care.

This philosophy reads two sections, an explanation and a warning. Please use these sections as a guide for living; they will aid the progression of your life and Our Plan.

Section 1: The Philosophy

'In the terms of social recognition,
communal cognition,
argumentative ammunition,
and relation nutrition,
please hide your talents, expertise,
or knowledge of any plenitudinous kind.
This is for the sake of
your peers or companions
you have any relationship with to feel
compelled to state the
equal grounds your feet are pressed
against,
albeit the fictional and cryptic
equality exposed here is
more obvious than not.
We advise you to cozen the
UFP's (Unreal Figments of Perception)
in order to reveal your life's meagre
benefits,
and to enable the development
of Our Plan.

Remember, you are not a
UFP, those who follow
the vague guidelines of simplicity
are considered the title.
Do not feel threatened by the name.'

Section 2: Warning

'If ignored or misused,
a prosecution of one extent
shall be placed.
In ignorance, you alter the progression
of Our Plan.
Be aware,
this section is built with borders,
those of which are sheltered from
trial, court, or any
judgemental proceeding which may
give you less or more of an opportunity
than our own prosecution.
Acknowledge this instruction
but follow the philosophy.'

If you struggle to comprehend the contents of the sections, visit your local Perception Administration Structure or any subsidiary organisation of The Perception Administration; they will provide simplified explanatory instructions and guidance for you.

Thank you for your patronage to Our Plan,
The Perception Administration.

Winter on the Isle of Thaw, Part One: Thursday's Dusk, Middle Wind, Early Winter

Any above behind the compliment
of flapping disarray.

I heard the sound
from my cave,
the ways of chiselled timing.
I saw the mountain,
the peak,
it did through corners.
Halls and mourners,
but the dusk was when they wore
black.
I heard the sound
into my ears,
canal of white noise,
lake-flutter chirps of passing,
orange-time.
I saw the mountain,
peak of snow-helm,
control of flaking.
The raining years, thorough,
in royal deception.
The night sought cover
to shelter me.
I thought I had suffered
on great ridges,
I know.
Grass smooth,
the hum of the sky
at blizzard notation,
reminisce, I commit.

The blonde tones fell upwards,
direction of them,
the cloud-dwellers
and the duelling fool.
I held upon a banister
of boulder conquest,
the resting leaf dies
in artificial plantation,
polished in an acidic zest.

Dusk of Thursday, I read,
breeze chilly, ready for a new day.

Winter on the Isle of Thaw, Part Two: Friday's Dawn, Flame Rest, Again, Winter

I cracked out,
ember.

Broken amongst the whispering
edge,
bleeding, the gaseous warmth.
Outer, nerve-connected
and stretching slowly,
in rocking and wheels, back
to the forward location,
then backwards once more.
Intentional?
There were causes of nipping
ears, they once heard
frost to be deafened by
the same tones.
My face rinsed
in clot-colour,
abstraction from the escaped
bargaining,
contribution through charity,
a funeral is not charity.

Charred, my new form
of liquid skin.

Winter on the Isle of Thaw, Part Three: Winter's Flurry, Hurry Now

Peach powder of grain,
skies shivering softer.

Expansive,
larger than what defines the term,
mid-winter, the gloom
of mild lust, they placed
celebrations to dispose of the
cooler fears.
I moved to valleys of tracks,
made,
where the buffalo and
the bull stood,
in the yarn of the ocean.
Once more, from
salted engagement,
the iris gallons flood,
boasting the turquoise
presence of before,
if you could remember.
I possibly contain the tinge,
slight tracks made from ...
The rose rain,
how it leaked from calmer
scalp to scalpel incision,
on my clasped palms,
dressing the
outskirts of my
city collection.

Hydrochloric silk,
I sighed with each wave,
if they had contained chlorine,
the substitute, in reference
to This Scenario, and
This Scenario's zinc.
I had not
gathered clothing,
the prepared items,
just the
singular wish.

The helmet of human quality, found
in my compassion for an
unreachable heat.

Teachings of Continuity, Part One: Like an Anthill, Progression

Pull the mound,
strive in gathering,
we push our instructing,
the equivalent of crown-possession
guides us,
eat, then sip on cane.
Energy in compost,
our ecosystem is maintained.

Pull the mound,
strive in gathering,
I push my instructing,
she instructs me,
but she thought not of me.
Eat, then sip more.
But no more than that?

I know,
I exist in this worthwhile scene,
short, acknowledged by my
time.
What if cane could be water?
Water to cane,
the dining trial of
twelve, seemingly,
hours,
prior to hill
embellishment.
What if dull paste could live thoroughly,
down through me in more hydration,
not of sweetness but of rejuvenation?

Pull the mound,
I told her,
in fact stood on
aforementioned hill
pride,
and preached,
but did they stop for me?
I imagine
if we were in the same,
as I,
this colony.
Would it fall?
What caused me, Antheim Schurly,
to walk from tunnel to leaf,
and leaf to tunnel?
And, I spoke the words, taking
no interruption,
in that.

Pull the mound.
But I stop, what is the exhaustion,
as is simply thought,
lack of thought drives me
less than thoughtlessness.
I do not fly and strive,
grow wings,
make a hive.
I pull the mound.

Teachings of Continuity, Part Two: On Living, and The Living

I sleep,
wake from slumber.
It is confirmed in daily hesitation,
that I will sleep tonight.
Somewhere,
the duvet painted in small ruffles,
the ink washing on my face,
where one could read
about seven, in morning
compartmentalisation,
the news of the prior day,
maybe.
Or open to find,
door of heaviest whisper,
like a sigh,
my belongings were lost.
I slept
on the contrary,
and had risen again
like a park-bench priest
of reincarnation,
I thrive in the tomb that is
this punctured-palm
civilisation,
obeying the murder
of nettle-precedent.
What if, one day,
I wake down,
to return differently?
If there is a return,

if return is the turning point
to decipher,
I have watched the crushed
night-fly,
several months ago.
It has yet to be returned,
yet to decompose,
yet to flinch from the
very same corner,
of the tile wall.
I capture, in thought,
myself flying,
happily and without
mind to buzz into
by-stood window
creek,
the falls of the spiteful grey
resistance,
they crawl like the fourth
year a baby spins,
underneath the hooves of
freight trains.
When descending from flight,
I squawk in fear and
die without a thought once
for my care.
I walked by a petal garden,
dumbfounded of
prepossessing pollen,
synchronised air
and caterpillar waltzing,
in their cocoon.

To the gnarly shattering,
holding more thought
to the pressure they move
that soft skin,
potential for kindness,
I am eliminated.
I had executed such passion of
execution to
the night-fly,
so I am not mistaken,
when they come from
the land of
ascension,
the only moment they descend,
the very same time it is
they come to eliminate.
What lives?
At the present moment,
it is eternal.
If it were eternal,
my conception and elimination,
I find I long for a
noticeable revive,
I die eternally,
for eternity?
I also live my strength and
rest-needed times,
in the same length as my
elimination.
Of the living, I give
a gift to hopeful
receiving.
You,
and to only you.
What will you live for in eternity?

Teachings of Continuity, Part Three: Socket Sickle

Plugged, you had it
separating in irony,
despair,
and totalitarian
collectives,
the spark lighting and quark
altered savages
you governed,
screaming in repeating tones,
distorted vowels,
and consonants,
consistently prying,
you made into
their being,
ran through legislature,
chained up with the shackles
of your socket sickle.

What named,
reaping to sow,
and taking alternatives,
the amount of excess into the
second-handed,
down from and
inheritance,
the ultimate of passing by,
the passing of equality and its
solvent mixing.

Set on nearer to the
up-window of midnight star,
to only five held in Butterscotch,
to dress in such does not
correlate to its taste
because
Butterscotch can also run late.

Souls of Samsinagro

If you pass the trees
of the lost words
from the sad people
that illustrate their
peaceful misery,
you will come to find
a town of desert-attitude
and caress their forlorn
wishes with lights hindered
by fumes.

The souls of Samsinagro
were tearful in the night,
crawling to a bliss
imprisoned by a carefully
placed blight.
Hold the souls from the grains,
count them individually
and see that each sadness
filled the oceans of
pain.

The village or the town
pillaged by frowns,
impoverished, they stood
and famished, only they could
have seen their dissipating
deception from
lunar representation,
that midnight boulder,
a toddler on the horizon

and the crystal warning
which sat on the eye-split
of the oasis
sang the memories
of the forgotten.

And the souls of Samsinagro
were hidden away,
a key that corroded
on the slumber of the sea waves
with echoes of the dripping sighs
flooding the cheeks
of the land with a
teary demise.

The clouds were to come
as if they were crowds,
or bouquets of shrivelled
leaves and parades
of bees,
honey-hungry knives,
the wives of Samsinagro
were perspicacious of their
belittling survival,
the husbands were to
grow in a venture
of war, but the children
fell to a decline,
yes,
the children failed
their dismal life.

The souls of Samsinagro
enraged in red and indigo
of scarlet dresses
and black umbrellas
in the storm of
thieving authority
had precipitated its
condolences on
this settlement,
the priority of
the town died
in mediocrity.

The country once prospered
with golden shrubs
and the bushes of factories
reaped the bullets of diamonds,
the bulbs of stars, and
the tint was orange,
bright and honest,
a worm beginning
for the owl town in
the tree country.

The souls of Samsinagro
were penned in the books
with a charcoal ink
made from the logs of their wood
and a container for the ink
from their cancer-ground sand
completely burning in fractures.

Feathers of the crows
would soon show in the
branches, while a country
born of spirits-good would
be rich and ripe in spirits-bad,
and the snow of the particles
of a numb, soft-touched apology-stack
wound-stitched the hills
of a town in black.

And the souls of Samsinagro
would shatter an hourglass
through a timely attack
of a seated desperation,
and the spines of the backs
of the people's participation
snapped like the coal
of a flame.
The town snapped in
the country of shame.

The orange,
the brightness would soon
bleed with a lack
of colour
and of health,
and of a golden wealth,
where the oceans would
drown in the dehydrated rivers,
the cold town shivered
and silenced.
The cold town shivered
in violence.

The souls of Samsinagro
had lived in the aching
of a drumming pitch,
of a labour,
of a pestilent dishonour they
perished in erosion,
distinguished, yet thrived
and the bell-tower rings,
alive.
The bell-tower signalled
to the town, a dive.

The mountains around
would collapse,
a crown of a ruby blood would
relapse in a topaz torment,
the mentality of the citizens
refrained
from movement
through the sights
of a final window dove.

The souls of Samsinagro
flooded with hatred,
they gazed at the
embers of control,
they knew once again
a hope had vanished,
all to live through
a cracking window pane.

I walked by the walls
of green ivy, frost, and
moss
and found a lost diary
of words, of loss,
so I took it from the urn
of this old family life
and gave the pages
a turn.

But the souls of Samsinagro
had pierced my silver eyes,
of jewel graves
and lives saved
by an anguish-delight
and prepared me
to read with caution,
to erase my judgement
through experience.

"To live in anger
is to die in freedom,
a baby born
was an ignorance, turned.
May I die like the dove,
over there,
on the cross-stump
dressed in nail-laces
and love."

The souls of Samsinagro
had glistened in my thoughts
like pearl-murders hanging
in the throats of
the forgiving
for they forgave in
the desire of
an opportunity.
They waited for
a new chance to hate.
A bliss in the splitting
of fate.

Soul Rent, Part One: Laced with Silver

Chrome adorned,
searching,
I had been, for
life's inglorious cycle,
of a price not to have
been paid.
If I were to be the
insatiable leech,
after the inherited death,
I am sucking,
in fact gulping,
the discovery of prime quality,
and if you have to search for it,
the slim rarity it is the
chance that whatever
is laced with silver,
maybe, there is not a
piece of silver to be found.

Soul Rent, Part Two: Costing Not a Penny

To inch away,
sooner,
no limitation of prevention
could provide the highest,
their boundary of exchange,
leads to plummet,
the summit of anticipation is
the ignorance
of the ending.

Such sequel would come
after blind memory,
or blinded,
to whichever
process occurs,
may there not be
proof that exchange is futile,
such design creates ancestry
prevailing
immensely vaster
than any bloodline,
to the moment,
this,
and copper couldn't save you.

More than a Mark

Mileage remaining: that of ... thirty-nine.
Pacing on the stainless angles of the fainting
was a male of induced labour.
He, boot-strapped in a regulatory guiding,
enabled in clarification,
stable, next to the station,
doubled flaxen strips,
waxed tips,
addressing lips,
lawful divorce.

In his abstract pockets of alpaca fur,
or down-forth and under, naive underlining,
silk, rayon, needles, and two
dove medallions, brass.
Awaiting the shopkeeper's
arrival, he embraced reluctance
to reveal his sentiment; kept talents, and
proclaimed they were for home-time relations, wife.
He never married for he never
felt the colliding attraction, only the stagger
of the sewing machine kept those darted eyes
in the cinnamon rays.

An evening tiptoe by the city,
entrance to the neon patch.
Was it, life, ever as dull as this?
He parted from his overcoat
of beating stability
and hung it like
conscious pork on flames,
over the
familiar metal-bends.
The factory vibrations
ruptured the directions of the wind,
hence why he felt a drowsy gale
of heat.

Mark, his name had to be shown,
happened in cotton and yet to be sewn,
stitched up in bleeding velvet
in the mattresses of his mind,
matrimonial detriments
and parental influence, behind.
He was more than a Mark,
more than simple,
betraying his shackles,
silver and chrome;
in productivity,
activity, anticipation,
and,
action!

More than a Mark,
just an ordinary Mark,
he made more of a mark
than any extraordinary Mark
because he, himself, was extraordinary.
More than a Mark,
he resides there, Mark,
an oak tree of nettles and bark.
Oh! Mark,
your time, nigh,
destination, arrived,
kingdom on high,
cloudy shrouds of disarray.

Mark, you have made one,
of course,
but in due course,
you have ran our course,
vocals, hoarse,
like a distressed horse or a freshly formed hearse,
you work in death and slumber in life.

May you rest.
'At ease,' read your stone,
'Rise soon, fall now,
kindness, remember, never acts.'
Read once more, 'It is only implied.'

Love at the Cann in 2007, Part One: Bingo and Joe

Bingo! Said Joe,
Oh, he did not know,
the rules of this game were played
in the inebriated sense,
no sense,
nor cents to play with,
the scarf, ultramarine,
and dull blood stains,
the blotchy tidbits of the sane,
laughing concoctions of
water blasting,
everlasting, cigarette
fighting and jarring,
sparring, the bar filled with
the people of motivation,
relevant to their sides, buttered
and feelings, fluttered.

Joe!
My cup, please.
The train soft and my time,
through the loft,
up and down,
not a frown in the hour
of waking, I whined.
Chasing a bit,
the train,
its wheels,
clicking and thudding
and stained mahogany,

I step into the leather booth.
There I found the Joe,
or mosaic decor,
it was not a bore
in my not-so-late snore,
and my evening stood upon
hill destiny.
Chilly and cool,
I read my paper,
confounded and anxious
at the latest
road-basher, placed it on
the pull-out desk,
the Sun fainted harder
on the Moon-painted
sky,
and only left asking,
my, oh,
I,
had I?
Had I left the cup to cool down?
I got off at the station,
in my contemplation
and confusion,
emotion of my thoughts,
I directed my hair behind
and headed southbound
to the nearest
coffee-house in the land.

Bingo! Said Joe,
again this time too late,
in this newer
talk-stating he refrained,
stuttered and
still remained that,
like a pill,
crushed and admired like a
saint.
So Joe,
in his boots or stilts,
did he move,
half a limp in his step,
bog-yellow, his coat,
from walking it would float,
in his talking he would bloat,
tripped and tumbled to
Morgan's for a sip.
The night prior, his wife,
Lenny Loxen, left
him and stole his heart,
he slung and he slurred as
the sugar would be stirred.
"An ungrateful coward, she was!"

I walked into fine presentation
and greeted a
misinterpretation,
left the station behind,
my mind
on hind legs,
kicking and
in formal begs I asked
for a latte to leave.
A sad man named who?
I did not ask,
nor did not want to,
clearly a wreck
similar
to a country surrounded in
ammunition,
where there were more
bullets than enthusiasm.
He invited me over,
I changed my small order,
replaced the drink into
a long glass,
and Joe,
now I know,
his story,
history,
we made.
A life to throw,
I held his hand and
endured him so,
like parting ecstasy
with the
Queen of Hearts.

Joe said to Bingo,
he followed her with her name,
she fled from liquor dreams
to follow,
what it would seem,
the fountain of business,
so rough.
She felt more intrigued
and Joe told her wisely,
"Come home with me
and enjoy your time,
in a cappuccino of a
bigger size."

I guzzled like mouthwash
the latte of hogwash,
swapped with a cappuccino
for two.

And Bingo and Joe
left to an apartment
in Soho,
the highest one, great for
a view.

Let us look soon
a bride and a groom,
but friends
not of London descent,
the city's jest,
more tales of
an interrelated interest.

Love at the Cann in 2007, Part Two: Lenny and Brock

Up in the woods of Canadian clashing,
a hunter and his husky,
very dashing.
Brock stood up to the sound of a
fox,
or a wolf, or even a pup.
So with his rifle, took aim,
a new trifle for dinner,
how Brock would be the winner,
of bread, of breed,
the wind thinner,
and richer, became that of this
trigger-twitcher.

I stalked up the head of a mountain,
my name,
Lenny Loxen,
up did I trail the beating steps,
for now I would rest,
a fire, at best,
next to my thick tent,
and nearing sleep.
In the next morning,
in peripheral circumstance,
sluggish and slain,
was I,
daffodils and daisies and
white-haired mazes
of rabbit-hat magic
habitats.

Brock Follen,
fallen against the
greatest stretch of
Alaska's border,
but he knew to stay closer
to water,
waiting, he had been for
the next sacrifice,
divine, utterly nice,
cooked perfectly with
salt and rice, he would
chop it, then dice,
steam it, the meat, thrice,
and part some in favour
of his white paw-pouncing
fellow.
Follen and Fellow,
soon with a lock to tie,
a Loxen third to complete
the word, the phrase of
Lenny and Brock.

Upon the rocks, I stood nearer
to hydration,
leather and rubber lasted my feet
to beat,
hypothermia, thermal,
the heat had not dropped,
but snow, the brightest foe,
Sahara, opponent, opposed no
threat to this challenger, I placed
my odds in
a bet, to race from the Sun,
to the abandoned silhouette,
the cabin-like structure
in a pine population.

Brock and his Fellow,
Follen so mellow, a conversation
was all he needed,
remembering Bingo,
and her friendly lingo,
he knew she had to go.
But noticing now,
the village hidden in
the clouds,
Follen locked eyes on Loxen.

I debated to run,
but what I now know
was fun,
I ran to old-man Brock.
Ten feet apart and a
poisonous dart,
the aim of his shooting fear,
unbeknownst to my identity,
at this time both of
us in dual curiosity,
I walked to the tip without fear,
strolled with my hips and told
Follen to follow me.
I set up my tent once more,
relentless, so content,
he caught his prime meat
in the midst of the
coolest afternoon.
We prodded and we steamed,
boosted self-esteem, and
spoke wisely of partners
of the past.

So misconstrued was Joe at the
apartment,
Loxen had to leave
in sorrowful means, he wanted to stay at
Morgan's Muffins and Lattes,
played in his sadness, like the mouse.

I headed for Canada,
my life, nearer,
Brock listened closely and
sympathetic he was,
to the woman who fled from
the lands of union.
Brock spoke of Bingo
and her timing, fatal,
she desired London,
I came from there!
Loxen and her swaying hair,
answered Brock's swift notation.

They hunted and thrived,
so bold, so alive,
living together
in the new millennium,
and its beginning.
Soon, however,
near a decade late,
a tale of Southern England.
A surprise would be found,
Loxen, Follen,
history in the kingdom,
united.

Love at the Cann in 2007, Part Three: The Cann, Once More, in 2007

Back in Southern England,
roughly ten years forward,
admittance of youth
at the wooded reservoir.
The many-legged
specimens hung from
hallucinogens, the powdered
spray of bell plants.
Intermingled tales,
predicted Ula the Teller,
Brandy the Willing, on the other hand,
had never expected such
a showing representation
of failure.
They scribed rusted battalion
on the sign of the nature reserve,
two hearts in the Cann,
next to a river
of soil-hue,
missing the limited experience
yet to view.
Ula told of cafeteria expression,
mountain-doused era
and exploitation.
Brandy held Ula in the
palm of his hand,
Brandy would tell Ula
of his snow-roasted demands.

Some of which included the experience
of two thousand,
some of which included the
having of a tulip-laced land.
Ula explained of his foreseen
betrayal,
stranded, was Brandy,
at the end of the
pebble-trickled trail.
Brandy harassed the air
at which his voice grew,
and passed the signature of
oxidised atriums, two.
But nowhere had found
Brandy unto Ula,
for Ula's experience,
thirty years at the smack
of the hands.
Had Lenny, Brock,
had Bingo, Joe.
his mind on the mushroom
motorway,
their loving unknown.
What played next, the
reel to Brandy, his
cinematic mind.
In the throne of ivy-stained furnishing,
he tripped and he stumbled,
passing the cobbled memory,
seen,
at last he had launched
like the Sun's daunting gleam.

Escaping the paradigm,
the swirling tie-dye,
in his void-expanding eyes,
how they travelled across
from each other, he
did not know the link.
Brandy had known Ula, the love
dissipated in
a blink.
“Brutal, inhuman experience!
You’ve guided me here,
without sense.
I waited for Ula and betrayed her
similarly,
the heartfelt trial
of the quartet of
familiarity,
false, my consequence.
It was all in years,
ten,
but minutes ten only?
My mind vast,
my heart, lonely.”
He rolled out of his
lucid nightmare,
hesitated,
he hadn’t,
stalked the rail of pain,
never to arrive at the Cann again.
He had not noticed
after walking by the sign,
There, the insignia!

The love at the Cann in 2007
was real,
almost as blessed as the water,
into the sacred wine.
If you do not look,
the objects not seen
do not exist,
to Brandy, this
Cann adventure,
it was
a cannot.

Incense's Sediment of Discernment

The seeing, most cruel,
in any rapid standard,
their deception heightened
with concentration
most thick,
any velvet compassion,
their vessels, burgundy
like leather engagements,
a pale marital engraving
on a ring of crimson flushing,
a brazen trust,
they trod the memorable aisle,
a garden of
visor-covered
blindness.
The sheen,
an assertive benediction,
blessings by a
desultory sacrament,
transfigured and present,
feelings, effervescent,
the timing of the
Senior Swallow
and her harsh crackle,
the piercing cackle had
risen with the
seeded bodies,
six prior to the noon
happenings,
I glance from my restless
morn
I did, to the decay of a
fateful falling.

Born chlorophyllic, the sky
now bronze,
its copper entwined
curtain lace
like any warm ray,
if only deception,
a core embellishment
to the salvation
of a forked leaking,
the primitive
refuge,
hospitality of criminal hypocrisy.
Hunting again, the
Senior Swallow
towards planet movement,
named purely,
'Incense,'
for her
vapid silhouette lingered like
foresight,
nonsensical, her stinging
flight shook away like
scavengers;
the gull noise,
dull
but impactful,
the corrosion of lungs settled
on cobbles in tobacco
levitation,
urn-ash contemplation.

The temptation
to get the better of her,
I attempted flying in
a sarcastic detriment
unbeknownst to my person,
on such an authoritative
craze, the
lazy haze
of this societal collapsing.
Extension passing the communal
history,
only on the topic
you guess my tongue,
alternatively I wade
through tsunamis of
false judgement
and only found in
my dearest cartography,
the coastline of erosion,
currency of severed exchange,
slashing the Saturn,
the satin
with any parsley touching,
turning the page,
they ignore finite
wage,
the infirmary of pain,
again,
in shades of criticism only
in the pronunciation of
colour, the misguided assumptions,
prior settlements
of colloquialism, aneurysm,
mysticism,
with this delicately placed tangent.

Incense! I screamed,
your breast of life's whitest,
tone so pure,
altered not.
Do I need more?
I desire in that
aforementioned purity,
of any indoctrination
willingly sour,
like eighty-three enhancements
in the singular
coruscation of guidance.
Guidance you need,
well, Incense,
I may show you the
encapsulation of sight,
blind Incense,
I may portray the times,
deaf Incense,
you may fly without
feathered limitation,
stripped in
the Magdalene latex farming,
canonical speaking
to Iscariot precedent,
the lucidity of
imagination,
Incense,
I may tempt you forth
in a scaly-brick
serpentine speech.

Oh, Incense,
so you gulp,
so you hesitate,
your ultramarine
weight,
the passage of iris staring,
Theia cursed, the
pavement on your holding,
sweetest Incense,
flights and tales
of curtailed cutting,
the chamfered corners of ease,
like a preacher who portrays
fictitious knowledge,
the dirty, raggedy, pavement-Messiah,
on his knees,
a kingdom of peasant-presence
upon clouds daunting this
harrowing slavery,
fault of experience,
praised of utmost allegiance
to simplistic insight.
Length may not prevail
but length may tell,
any hindered, kindred
ember of an
amber-waxed refining
of city soul,
the lake twining far and
a farce, calling from
branch song,
only Incense,
her lustful cranium,

estranged under the
infrared distortion upon
neon treasure.
Now, from mortar perspective
I hunt her outline as she
did to crescent motivation,
that spiked
persuasion,
defeat of many magpies
to her true
intention,
if only facts could be witnessed,
opinions swept under
kitten-paw scratches,
bacon-snout greed,
the snaffle,
the viral conglomerate of
wrath on to any who
dares prevent completion.
I knew progression
in conspiracy,
in rebellion only the
incremental progress would align
like solar perfection
against any governing.

Vernacular monstrosity,
I brand like the cattle-breeding
significance, the numerical
indentations swiftly deplete
origin's importance,
never do they encourage misalignment.

Solemn Debt Entourage, Part One: The People of Barbara Square

City centres,
its waist, the outskirts of
development-limited
in the cross-point,
sharper than sight;
bladed perception to conjoined
and planet-binding presence,
director to power aloof.
Shattered crescent,
crater present,
hidden below
blown horizons of captivity,
the brain projection to destination,
if only normal, considered following
having a destiny.
In which, theme conducts
the orchestra of titian embers,
the satsuma rise, sphere
to atmospheric impounding,
as ink couldn't replicate.
Letters, addressed to the alphabetical
means of organisation,
at which ruled my imagination,
conveyance of the fool,
the assumption of survival
plays on routine.
Nutrition salvaged,
the playground of disease,
hours passing,
cured in cellular depreciation,
and chamber wither.

A man and only one
had owned
the shafts of the bank's mines,
he ate labour and spat gold,
the diamond pavements foretold,
the stepping,
heading-way to his maintenance.
Sustained in whiplash patronage,
the wheat, warm, in
coal-fire blankets,
dry, more than any tear to pamper the
skin of the sublime,
luggage exoskeleton, its taste,
vibrating inner sense,
the innocence of teaching.
A man,
and only one,
wrist-laced leather if the cow
was considered conscious,
the slithering,
considered trustworthy,
the paddle,
considered reliable.
Seagulls dressed in green,
starving like dehydration,
graced in their moss-harbour trust,
multiple flags,
the sleek mannerisms of the
yacht sails.

You could wear any and all colours,
unnoticed by the security observation,
their operation of hind mentality,
their fractures begging
the prior abilities,
they become disabilities.
A nest of them perched in the
metallic submission,
two branches to the layered sponge;
not-so-greedy sponge,
floating about
like the fin of a shark,
boarded temptation,
jaw to propose to
inflatable bakery,
pastry of moist foam flesh.
Down,
the perspective dweller,
miles from you longs loving,
the ant on dead paving,
your sandal stench infuriates
the foul inscription,
the toned and
padded landing.
Gaze at me with odd obsession,
dire event in question, my being,
closely present and
the only present entity
in your aura is ignorance.
Scatter, hence elder,
government collision
has arrived.

Harrowing, stern,
stupendous;
inebriation, but of power,
I beg to exhale you from my radius,
in pearlescent sneezing,
from century strength
for you to proceed in consequence,
once more.
My attention next to bars,
needing painted banquet;
bouquets of floral insecurity lacked
the chamber of
entity judgement.
Or boundary,
our need to move forward
is rattling in the
vibrations of emotion,
so strenuous, swallowing whatever
energy remains
of the corpse.
Dotted about,
rings to aid the drowning,
the cheeks,
the photographer's dream,
of capturing substantial motion at
a freezing moment,
stationed in metaphorical attitude,
you would not struggle in wanting.

Bleak slugs in the commandment
of false words, the shores
of people,
crowds,
spread from the almighty delusion.
Slowly I tilt cranium weight,
curious skull,
to keep stranger-man in frame,
it could have been
'Only one,'
I knew it was
'Lonely One,'
but
'Lovely One,'
the phrase of maternal ringing,
if I greeted these words
without greeting,
I never would have found them.
Peaceable socialites,
their pretend sniffing,
like hound curiosity;
cats never dared.
Hinder my silence, I will retaliate
in threat
to your hesitation.
Saturday chuckles;
your breeding assumptions,
limited to
the behaving foresight,
white cloak
longs for cloak-none friend,
I studied such a notion months prior,
blessed white cloak.

Blue garments wore cloak-none,
the fascination stitched in the
intervening of
omnipotent whistling,
simply blue garments to cloak-none.

Mistaken folds,
I will befriend you,
any other way of the path,
tell him,
your staring, obvious,
his noticing, oblivious,
if you delay more,
your memory will twist
like the rounded telling of nursery
confinement,
toddlers bound to the
porcelain horses of the time.
Affairs, events,
we are such;
buckled.
His puddle limp has inspired this
sentencing to midnight,
ribbed ego, flying
in gaseous atomic pattern,
tinted lemon,
resting on the blonde-clear
figure, tell-tail-tied,
headed to the races.

I see the topaz-neck,
the wing-squandered
child landing the final placing,
of reminiscing,
to review similar
scenario,
I proclaim,
"Excellent effort!"

The hopes of hapless appreciation
to my commenting,
the steam houses piping away,
the person of the sky
collapsing,
both interest and physicality
dissipating like prism sight,
signs ensuring noticing
toward distanced dismay,
happen, now, exhaustion.

I hadn't noticed, colour
in electrical ray,
the rails
happened upon a bunch,
they walked, weary,
on iron trails,
with nothing but sarcasm
in their raspberry munch.
Defenestrate the room,
she decided,
but not of any object,
if of course you believe
that person and actuality
cannot be objectified.

Among the sewer avenue,
her fears and crimson tears magnified,
what mattered,
only the flowers of
the balcony presentation.
Fun, false, in
due, set date of monthly
overthought,
where commitment is dreaded,
marriage causes worry.
Caught with red hands,
the crab of nettle sympathy,
coldest of feet;
temperature, the ultimate effect,
the temperament of miniature
betrayal.
The settled future, wiped from
vision,
I altered time at blight.
I reunite with the dawn,
bed-wake, the coffin of true rest.
Frosted pane,
multifarious caffeinated memories
perfected the charred shelves of cigars,
the fine grain of the dream.
Hint of chocolate, dash of
pepper,
symbolism to the sweetest
sorrow of living.

Caused at the opportune,
and without resistance,
moment,
blaring,
the irises of the mysterious
intrigue,
I plead to exchange
misery,
salvation is wasted on
the city's seventeenth-floor
mistrust,
the corridors of capitalism,
their flaming brass knuckles
to the bones of misfortune.
With essentials limited,
happiness is found,
my only company
is the decay of moth debris
upon frail realisation,
chimneys were the lungs
to the cigar-steam
they abolished.

'Lonely One,'
I am labelled,
unstable to building
ownership, I fret to
inform listeners around,
my ownership of
your lives,
a regret I hold once more.
In unison,
may you shine brighter
than the fractures most dim,

most pale,
in wicked longevity,
rendition of schematics,
to disappointment,
distasteful, mild,
mild is not total elimination.
Forgettable impatience,
signified the proletariat;
singular among peers.
Known only to self,
hence left of thought,
one.

Praise, the fountain of obligation,
I tremble from their stepping
interruptions, or eruptions,
the ripples of feigned fondness,
the triune deceit.
One of many,
twice of thrust,
third on the lacking wires of
chiming trust,
to which opportunity is
capable
without a hand to hold,
if all is taught that there are
available hands,
one would expect availability;
where guidelines exist
without a personal guide.

Aching wrist of lonesome
repetition,
the written conglomeration,
candidate to stressful
frustration.
From ochre to ginger,
thrice, again, repetition
of this fallacy,
petition, signed to allow
shallow hindering,
applied.
Ochre, the introduction to
never reside elsewhere,
I continue in
alternatives,
if my uncertainty is at
any accuracy,
the bridging
caricature of my naive trail,
righteousness found like
the rusted replacement of
oyster gems.
Shade of nostalgia,
painted in my forborne
longing, announced in silver,
polished in titanium,
commanded in stone
and sold in gold.

Continuation under categorical
value, I arranged fruition
in fortifying lust,
the superficial segmentation,
branches to the migraine named
roughly,
'Experience,'
at the forked tastes tapping my mind.
Infantile, now irrelevant,
the creation of the surrounding strain,
the grey of any gleam,
outside of existence,
the likelihood,
like any dream.
Rash, cinnamon,
of seedling intervals
any more detrimental
to imagination,
you were about this person,
I banished like crumbs to the
underworld of recycling, as any
other informative senior
may advertise as the
sacred selection,
I loved and executed with
a crumbled insight.
The blinded anguish to armies
of incredulous herds,
initiated in panic attacks,
the attack of shielded
tyranny.

The timely spoiling, from
opinion to viral conserves,
spread on like tar to
martyr fleas,
strictly to violet disguise,
and velvet disgust.

They took it like sugar,
expected like a cure,
the wrath of approval,
fainting,
it ended the misguided
and ill intervals.
Like all addictions,
just one extremely falsifiable,
vinegar told to be juice,
they believed,
reading fruit.
The committed fraudulent temper,
the tempest of the short term,
dwelling on moment
to expect desire,
quickest, the load
thickest comes to those
most crooked,
orchestrated incorrectly,
branded sociopathic,
another quality to linger.

Quarterly marital positivity,
red-breasted robins to propose
the vain finger you now
aim on this facial target of
my own.
I am no jewel,
a prize, considerably,
though, at
the hypnotised,
found in the dirt,
an undesirable fragment of
plastic dressed in the
pyrite of persuasion,
further carries
the mileage of temperament,
held closer than giving,
you gave me to
a constructed soil.
Running to familiarity,
the squid
to my lost octopus,
the empirical triplet
of amusement
to find the roles reversed,
of course,
if any were to remain.
The foe of highest tempo
speaking like a
book's legacy,
once deceased
at a plank,
its arrangement,
and a craftsmanship to
spite in aluminium freedom,
cruel objectification.

My fault,
like a prior sponge to digest
tsunami quantity,
that of your deluded empathy,
sheepish nature and
narrowing compression,
the altitude more cancerous than
any lung failure.
Perched in depths,
still screaming,
I broke loosely,
if bubbles were to carry bubbles
sentient enough to bestow
importance,
I was the only bubble you
shattered
that contained your vicious
tension.
The fearful agents
hidden in chemical irritation
alternate with visions,
the primitive escape to
evangelical living.
Irises were fixated with
prior notations,
the outstretched arms
tensed in spasms to
the out-of-reach distraction,
to only
lactic defeat,
they part
in an acidic tantrum,
the thinnest glass,
they shattered
with the whispers of truth.

Smallest town,
tears, scale-embossed
and refraction,
the visibility
from needle to stream of
drowning concoction,
the ambiguity
of miserable ticking,
entwining fate with
calamity.
Omitted like a limb
belonging to the
incorrect beholder,
way-forward,
halted to begging caller
of prior interruption.
The rapture of
assumed intention
beckons
my core to strangle only
my unwilling gestures.
Vacuous intent to
a hateful annoyance,
if only time were
to shatter immediately for the
purpose of materialism,
at only individual
moments of attention,
you!
The mirror of
hollow reflection,
intensity to the
rhythm
of a
baked neural interconnection.

Lime temptation,
endurance
to the
trident of acknowledgement,
denied by a
lonesome,
feathered sleeping.

Solemn Debt Entourage, Part Two: A World Most Cruel

Like a pebble,
falling through indigo,
train dragging misery, refined,
the scolding
reservation,
the production
of abrasion,
forward to bridge-parted
ending.
Proclaim your essence passing
conscious hours,
you caught me in
your netting, brushed like civil torment,
of charcoal carvings
and suicide.
What, only,
the conversation,
it never had me screwed,
the tightened mortality;
the duties of the people,
achievements,
beliefs and
fears,
the uninterested cavities
in my
severe altercation.

You seduced my artistic
cadence,
such stoicism I appreciated in
the approximate
seven towards your
one-and-a-half,
for only the time
to disregard me was the latter
on hour terms.
They fear eternal completion,
horrific, that of existential
questioning in the
most elaborate senses,
fearful of tangible perception
crumbling without real physicality,
unknown to their
sentience, the sentencing,
that sentient thought is calculated in
untouched, wired connection,
indistinguishable fanatics,
such as my own
questioning,
we reached interest
like vine nooses
in the strangulation of time.
I mourn over you,
for you have died in my
perception,
escaped, the prisoner of longevity
amongst the cascading
of such false physicality.

But, to hold you, in metaphor,
in prior seven speech,
the greatest hours spoken were
eliminated in your dismissed
actions.
Never, anyone attached themselves
like you,
I reminisce like the elder
of three royal cells,
encapsulating
hidden monstrosities of
their forsaken paths,
and on one inspiration
you stood with
a kitten of pregnancy,
immense want,
the sustenance,
with bile for
medicine you were
stricken down in discernment,
I linger in attachment
at the marital presence of
sorrow.
The proposal was
intriguing
but a wasting
time coruscated,
the rain of my
maelstrom eyes,
the cheeky slander
upon which spinning
takes his residence,
you were a boy of deepest
luxury, as
your luring,

daring,
flaunting,
what stole hindered eras
were unbeknownst to closest
of captivity,
your subtle reveal had me
trembling in your
doubtful lucidity.
The emblem gears of this
rod beseeched me
thoroughly,
a river inclined
to torment
the brook of my
skimming pages,
such was a biblical presence
capped like bullets,
they followed in the suspected
hyperactivity, in order of
awareness,
numerical, orderly in this
cruel devastation
I name,
'The Guideline,'
the aforementioned
resistance
to torched branches,
the blessed
gallows you mentioned
were of cubicle
ideology,
segmented
and
compartmentalised,
division in

civil equity,
I admire such gain
in speech,
when in reference you
protested, to pen
such an odd name.
A lying reveal?
If only you were to reach one day,
again, I would embrace you
like a Catholic
who carries the prejudice of the
Protestant.
Streaks, your own slitting,
quilted and
mentioned, implicitly
the killing was internal,
of constant, opinion-governed
truths told
more than foresight,
the blonde of
your caricatures,
black and white,
your disposition. I
long for your presence,
the embarrassment upon reading
do I state your
solidified
plasma attitude,
you are my rapture,
the presence of monotony
and her despair, your fateful gazing,
like the lightning bolt,
only the entrance to
innards I opened your gates,
if gates were like the ventricles,

your left ventricle I lay in,
hoping for duvet fighting,
I fly in your dove compassion in
my ruthless analysing,
the only such comfort of dealing
with requests of the
many diseases,
like a cancer waiting on its
nested hatching,
the anatomy of remaining
shared, you excel like
the governing,
you propose
anarchy.
Your sacred temptation,
generationally kindred,
I held each
prior in moments,
the compassionate
tongue, like
your flesh,
smoothest and
warm, the
softest acceptance
I grew fond of,
admired and
worthwhile,
you express such cruelty in your
ignorance.
The same morning spread,
you never slept like one
was convinced,
the most intelligent,
the consideration
you are the same as me,

omnipotent in many times
you live in the
moment of admittedly
frightful decadence,
as you once admitted,
if time were of
separation, how real this
place of inhumane
construction
would be.
Splitting in
romanticised conglomerates
holds an unaccountable merit,
the awarding bodies
of deprivation.
starved and passionate I exhale
textile fortune to your bed-riddance,
in which I ramble and
play, I
used to be with joy
until parting with this
remedy of
'mares.
Superseding
visionary excellence,
the pages written to compile,
collate your betrayal,
you will be remembered less
than twenty-four,
but in years remains your solemn impact.
For striving to see purity
hiding in
the guise of insecurity,
the luxury of
your futility,

seeking
the residence of below,
held in your imaginative farce,
I could knight
you in deception,
if the honour was in my condition.
The amalgamation of
desire undermines
such description,
if I could describe to you the
painted secrecy of your
misfortune,
I would craft each atomic
point
with the greatest precision,
if it meant to speak, to
seek a reply from your
unwilling silence.
Speak, I once proclaimed,
speak,
to me,
I,
needing to hear your voice of
written salvation,
the only conspiracy
I allow to infuse into
miserable living,
this grey evidence of
living,
the jugular incision of
leaves
fading brown, the slug-wit
on high,
the stairs of
cracking rumination,

an afterthought
of evidently cattle-grounded
understanding,
the pausing fret to your
blooming society,
hidden, again,
the toddler agrees,
but,
oh,
to hold you in
this erroneous
enterprise
of metaphysical
creation,
the creation of you,
in which only yearning
conversation
and partnership,
earning not,
insertion of the pineal
divulgence,
used in similar
utterances,
I would dance proudly with your
pedantry
if it meant the night could play
like the
recorded anomie,
only recapitulation,
unfortunately gambolling
is of longing
and hardship.
I would stroll any cavalry
sentry-pointed finger,

the amounting of
down-let person,
weary on this
midnight comfort,
you pacified me more than
the preacher at the door,
knocking in belief to spread
his good news
of yesterday,
outdated like the coolest
ready-made coffee,
the belongings of his nature,
blasphemous in the
injustices of towel-stained,
dirt promise.
What did the seeker behold?
Only the
chanting
of hall obedience,
this life treats the
people more feeble
than of sensation,
they fell
content in the
glamour of
Sun-shining,
how that was not satisfactory
if seen daily.
The gift of consciousness
written like a burden in the
categorical
hesitation of
progression, that
which I now have to search
the

analogous conversation in closer,
more
propitious speech.
You must know,
the imploding
charcoal sketches,
they paint the sky with
hues of transparent raining,
to which my eyes have let from your
mind's transferring,
they leak like
chlorine on scar,
to which scented
esteem burns more than
association with the fool,
to what you have
associated with me,
the purgatory of
doubled edges,
I painted,
you interpreted,
two participants are
the debris of companionship and
loving,
I shall find peace
in the doomed
resignation of life
underneath the cabinet-hidden
features I possess, obviously made
of the glass cabinet,
you,
the blackest of birds,
skies,
tornado tantrum,
your rough curvature

illuminates,
ignites the flaming sensation of whipping,
the cracking of coal,
in my spine
severed,
savoured,
the embers of such used
to craft concealed identity,
which I play the part in the
trial of this half-incarnate,
your true being.
Revelled, you had me,
in your tendon
combination,
locked away like chambers
of wine, mulled to the
captivation of taste,
you were like grapes under
the vine-labyrinths,
strangling my lungs with
weary interpretation.
Explication, beyond which
you cover your turtle
caricature.
You lay, consciously arrogant,
in the knowledge you do not have,
that caricature is all that
is left of you.

Lost Notes, Part One: Lost Notes of Thomas Bitter

You and I should not have
been so close,
the windows
and the tormenting
blind ghosts,
cold-cool drafting fortune
drips like
milk bees,
the nectar cows
upon the seas
of love.

Lost Notes, Part Two: Lost Notes of Timothy Sweet

Hedges of the flowers
dotted about like yachts,
the sails of mistresses
and feelings,
the caveats,
the rocky-harbour midnight
Moon,
the river sleeps at
noon,
the lunar secrecy
and the coffee-place
heaven
illuminates like
burning charcoal.
You and I
had something good,
something more than talk,
our conversation
stood,
our conversation
stopped,
for you made
the poor decision
to leave
after morn,

I lay,
awake,
in sorrow,
I mourn this horror
of waiting,
like feelings
that have died
on the Cross
of wooden lies.

Lost Notes, Part Three: Lost Notes of Theodore Sour

The hill stands so lonely
in the valleys of water,
the hedges whisper,
they are tainted
like acrylic, painted
with transparent
tears,
they scratch
upon seams,
it seems
as though
you are hidden
in your perfect structure,
your body
and your mind,
I wanted
to embrace your
capture,
your now
sour kisses
I long for,
but you have disappeared
like a dying sigh,
or the day
into the night.

Delicate Equinox

I want the roses
stationed in their lot
their scented person
hues of apricot
the permanence of most true
is where I find you
in the autumnal garden
of your delicate equinox.

Blizzard of glory
the bat will rest in the cave
the nocturnal dependency
wings, the stone waves
harmony in despondency
a flaunting of fame
the equator hands of the Capricorn
the Cancer's shame.

Splitting segmentation
on ending result
in control
punishment of smiting
pieces,
was I in none
but one's presence
of my own
tormented sweeping.

Shattered sapphire remnant
if compromise
was the succeeding
ordeal,
debacle of sentry-assignment
focused in tension of
cone disarray,
sacrificial enticement deranged on
interruption.

And the roses I wanted
were stationed at their lot,
the hues
more reminiscent
of an aching blood clot,
the tears,
they swell,
they rain on my locks
as I lay in this garden of
your delicate equinox.

Kitten Ends on Timothy

The dogs they . . .
They lost their branch squeal
like trees in
the autumn peel.

With snails in
and
kitten ends on timothy,
the only river swan
swimming
was the tearful
rolling,
the skimming pebble
from my
brook eyes.

I Walked to the Corner of Time

A written passage I grabbed from the gaping void of time's singular corner:

This is addressed to you, so keep this in your
mind's pockets.
My dialogue may alter preconceived
identifications, and limitation alters.
So what will you find in this haze?
Cosmic splitting matter; what matters is not
this. Of cognition, time begs for you to
understand and exist through its
construction; the result of these begging
periods includes and is limited to only
my acknowledgement of aforementioned
preconception. Time, the dictator of activity,
worsened by its everlasting reign; who
but my spoken words shall overthrow the
challenge of keeping you?

I have spoken this to you, exemplified by your
pictured aggressive tone you now read my peculiar
but smirking words. I now bark in denial, I didn't
know you would attach a voice! Time taught me
foresight. I will pause my conjectures, but understand
that conjecture is all you live through when
carrying the burden of time. Recycling like the
heavily choreographed swirl of
single-dimensional points, that I have reached abstraction
through this view.

Of comprehension, alternatively, I have confused you.
The third paragraph, in the order of the future following two
experienced and experiencing areas, you have tied the
familiar term of past beginning, for what began had
already happened. I have to ask the conscious thought.
In turn, please raise my voice in questioning pitch.
Another twenty-fifth, addressing the notion;
why have you thought in cyclical narration?

In what I have witnessed, time has been linked to the
clusters of subjects yet to be researched.
I propose a higher interrogation, and
under my arrogant knife I introduce
the proof of time disappearance. Everything
contained in existence is contained in
gifts and introductions. The present times are what we
observe in current moment, and in memory, we
know of the past. However, recording of memory simply
does not show the past, only the present exposes
reality.

The reality is that even records are present,
but experiences simply irreplaceable therefore
cannot be fossilised. An illustration of
the irreplaceable through the means of data
holds no equivalence, for even if the senses
were our approval that something was real,
time disagrees. At one time a present activity
occurs, it is irreplaceable simply because that time
has moved to a new time. Reproducing the
same activity in a different time is not
a replication.

A different feeling strikes through further understanding, as you analyse once more this line. What is reality if what is real is, in terms of time, irreplaceable?

Woman of the Blueberry Gabardine

The Sun
will set again,
a cycle I depend,
an ill end.

The weeds grow
from the concrete estate
and the boys,
knee high in white,
they beseech escape,
while any mother
scrunched their necks
and dragged them in,
the lamp light only
to see in the orange-black
gravel.

The Sun is beneath
a foot and a door,
the mistress
crawls beneath planks
of smoke,
she reaches for the insertion
in the
rufescent beams of temptation.

The boy had driven his route away to
some hostage bar for the naive,
he attached his
eyes on another
boy's rent,
for only
did they escape a
cupboard and a vessel of my intrigue,
seven later than intrigue met,
but I sipped into
my poison chalice
of sublime intention,
two glaciers amongst
smoky defeat
with their ashes falling down
into a glass memorial
of the addiction.

My leather in
the sea breeze,
a salt rain
poured over as I
watched them leave in
the drunk's chariot,
and the man-horse
begs for destination payment
but they stumbled into
position, rehearsed like
fumbling immigration
from a truck inspector's
false but seeing eyes,

where I lived in the
haunting sounds, long,
soon a flash would destroy
the night like a
French flag bleached in defeat.

She has eyes
like darts and to her dismay
her aim
calculated like tax,
unfortunately misplaced.
I saw the webs of his cranium
clicking from a reflection,
as his curtains undressed so
did his rose-beacon desire,
a bouncing wavelength
that coexisted,
never to coincide,
a temporary discharge
of particles within particles,
the failure of
a present embryo
distilled in anguish,
only me to find my
discrepancy in the
charm of hidden staring,
I cackled my
knowledge in the
horizon of the storm,
one of worry
that couldn't have met my
destroyed irises.

The chiming grows higher
and I am perched on my step nest,
the woman I held anger
was the only to appease,
in our bitter exchanges
I found a new fondness
for the woman of
the blueberry gabardine,
her buttons of reflection,
her under-clothes
of protection,
her silk on her earnings and
her lips in her pursed,
but her sulk on
my pout and
I reached out hungry for newer times,
hopefully she received an incremental
meeting of the minds.

I am obsessed
with her ego,
her narcissism is my lust,
I may creep around
like the beggar for
a twig of cocaine,
may her forest injection
be at my riches
and wealth for
a union
of meek will
and no hesitance,
she spoke casual at her mother
and her mother be of my presence
but her gifting entry

may speak
through my dimly sworn vision,
her swan immaturity
is my sheathing passion,
so she wrapped her bow
around her misshapen
figure and
would soon dive into the night
like a penguin amongst the cod.

He was far from my mind
could I only care for his disease
to be created in the chambers of
his shallow impression,
from the halls of nothing she was made
and the nests of everything
she may rest,
only my life's worth
to bury her in my breasted scenery,
and I refrain from meeting in the quartet
of futility,
yet when I hunt through
an unwanted mindset
do I crave
the most hated.

American Pestilence

Your mother
had died
one and one,
carbonated
stripes of the
free and none,
to Eastern
revenue,
the sparrow achromatopsia,
in support
for this
mephitic irony.
The pleasing,
iridescent,
acerbic judgement,
appointed
leech begging
to hinder
chilly wrapping,
harlot-spawn
offers
the
motherless impediments,
they pawn
the tendons
and soles
of escape,
the thighs
of rosemary sediment.

Pleased,
was I,
to find
you
strangled
and gasping
like moss
in
cumulonimbus pride,
to reside,
I then pounded
your fiftieth
dollar-coffin nail.
I sent you,
unleashed like
commitment,
like burgeoning
purges,
illusory urges,
I walked you
from your
blind-hound stepping,
you ceased
like freedom.
A wall
between
trick and mind,
what seems,
the years,
wastes
behind.

In anorexic betrayal,
they taper
into polygamy
like the communal,
air-soaring
traitor
of
kitchen-utility origin,
their umbilical
coordination to
the stainless twins,
some delivery,
they stood,
the apple
in a beggar's eye.
To watch a man
fall myths,
Zeus-high
and lifeless,
like
the apprehension
of birth.
I sit and wait
in my
sapphire cauldron,
I open,
by the day,
the harrowing
curtain laces,
longing
like homely
holiday.

I waddle
in capped-boots
unknowing,
I know,
I have
served
time,
but this maniacal
infrastructure,
only a displaced
rhythm
or
rhyme.
The butter
couldn't melt,
its refusal
to oblige,
like ledge-tripping,
the willing lie,
the pledged-whipping,
shot veins,
shuttle eyes,
turtle-throat noose
within
the mist of
sunrise,
in empathy
I watch them
wake beyond
my committing
discrepancies,
branded, cruelly and
from hatred,
wise.

I am the feathered
buffalo,
a figure of
thorn deceit,
horn-ring
marriage,
steamed,
and the shimmering
rosary
bleeds
with the
descending hands,
they slit the air,
they sleep.
Your mother
had died
one and one,
that casualty,
my misery,
your hapless
calling from
impossibility,
to say
my arms connect
would be writing
two thousand and one
April commands
to remember,
where blooming
would be delayed
to September,

misguided
semantics
and riddles
tracing your
blonde carcass,
the fond
affection,
I descry
your
American pestilence.

The Bag-Man and His Gin

Well I thought I saw the preacher
riding on his bike
he cycled up and down the street
and rested on his psych,
but he looked through and
down the alley,
wasn't a pleasant nature, he thought of
the two-lipped girl from the Town of Halley
and her apothecary layers,
the tall guy had walked in relapse
the small a tree-clasp attack,
a big-eyed disposition
and a bug-eyed tantrum disquisition,
my inquisition
a river's deposition,
the sea and the substation
the insect temptation,
but the town held protests
of payments reduced within,
the only man talking,
the bag-man and his gin.

I was stationed in my car
a leather dispatch and road tar,
I looked outside my window
to find a bus-man in the way
of views far and distant
of views frosted, in celibacy
they ricochet,
and a woman
on my left side
of a fox-rose and a thorn-frown
stitched me for a ride
and left me dead right there in Halley Town
wishin' for suicide,
my winter message
of teachings and deliveries
my solemn passage
of warmer memories,
the chimney chants and
the chimney screams
they once had
what the children dreamed
but reduction hadn't met next of kin
like the only man talking,
the bag-man and his gin.

The bald talent
and the bird's talons
they go around
the yet to be built blocks
they shy away on feathers
lost
they only hunt in flocks,
and much like the flightless
birds,
a repetition of arguments
from the feline-ultimate swerve
a gesture from ligaments,
and a subtle nerve
the beggar
he cries
in change and cups of tin
but the only man in the
silent town who was
talking
was
the bag-man and his gin.

Oh, the words of decks
and candle embers
a warmth, a peck
a chicken-oven remembers
on a lowercase number
nonetheless more numb
than the ferocious and dumber
there was a woman with a cherry beret
and another, a coat,
the only racket caused and smoked
livid and coaxed
and she is knocking
on the art store

to no avail
the post arrives an hour late
and she is left in the hail
without a canvas to paint on
she shivers in her ink
and watercolours of isolation
found
the bag-man and his gin.

The cherry beret grows stubborn
a mishandled credit debt
she is left away in the coldest bush
and with a poisonous regret
so she slams into the back door glass
of business and of fame
she gets the name of the haunting lass
unseen, ignored, she's outright vain
her cuts are my losses
of paints, of checking
in a French storm of agony, my pulses
are posted and stamped on
the glossy decking,
a balcony in the wind of the houses
a moose, a deer, a wreckage,
and the rat is let out
from the frigid factory maze
to come to find a snout
a-haze,
the governor snorting
staggered and stunned in Halley Town
by the only man talking,
the bag-man and his gin.

One More Rain

I'll say this,
for the times that differed prior,
they drifted for wishful humanity.
Imagine,
the star, it is to the progression
of immediacy,
instilled in delay before
continuation,
suffer, do we
to the halting of intellect,
the almost-getters
and the not-so,
the paper heads,
they frown in lines,
they sat with
smokes,
the rising
quivers and quenches,
I don't want to be here.
I am not searching for conquest,
only the new drizzle,
the distant wish
of one more rain.

You sit here on this bench,
if bench meant benches,
and you meant you-all,
that term, you,
my greetings of many,
the plural sanctity
of generalisation,
leaving breath, breathless,
where grains carry
plum-dotted umbrellas,
the judgement of
withheld jurisdiction,
like a candle
that cries in
the wax tyranny of flame torture,
the grasshopper lives in
a lovely place,
the grasshopper dreamt
of a lovely place,
the grasshopper kissed
Matthew's face,
the grasshopper upon and among
dreamer and dreaming,
tranquillity perished beyond
explicit intention,
so the grasshopper knew
hidden, blonde Matthew,
and Matthew prayed that sickening day,
where hands were nailed twice,
and again,
but Matthew and grasshopper,
he and they were such,
they both prayed
for one more rain.

Sandal-born and dehydrated,
happened,
the dizzy,
the demonstrated,
the recognised,
the circumstances
of regulatory eyes,
glass and false
they hang on poles
and meet you with clear
guessing,
and mask your fate
with second-messing,
and rip you a melody of numbing pain,
a destitution running late,
an entity of exchange falls with the
gasping desire
of one more rain.

Trains,
they carry me like mothers,
they left from sovereignty
to discernment,
but my expelling catastrophe
to the needle-shorts,
and the rusted clicking
of the steel miscarriage,
and temperaments,
I am offered a small satisfaction
and luxury of the tainted,
music of all
spoken to the wise,

the trains nurture from
London to France,
like a cufflink-hobo
who hitchhiked
from Soho to Penzance,
only the remaining clothes were woven,
with myths and stories
of catapults and glory.
The trains,
they'll tell you this,
"Our shelter warms you,
so sit tight for your safety,
it's cold outside,
it's chilly,
it's the wild captivity.
Our work
to deliver you from here to there,
walking, misleading,
following
but scared."
The trains,
they lie,
because shelter is temporary
and if you ever meet somebody
who claims the same game,
who acts like the train,
then only will you know
they long
for one more rain.

I hide my
belongings of feelings,
person and attitudes,
my mannerisms and
soul, the craft
embedded in the opinion
of strangers,
where one obstruction never seems
to fail,
the pattern of people,
they are repetitive
not-so curtailed,
for endurance,
my almost-got partner
between multiple recognition,
unnecessary to hope that
what they want to do,
the activity of basic
and of simplicity,
only those
were the songs of the coping.
The heavy and thick slopes
of summit greeting,
my exchange is yours,
so know
what belongs to you
because they will rob you like
pension
in the reckoning deceit of
expectation, a
payment to a day you do not
know your waking will
marry,
they will tell you
that you give them light,

they'll put you up on cross torment,
they'll ask for a fight,
they'll beat you down
with splinter-shackles,
they'll sing the psalms of spite,
and whisper the truths
of roads,
migraine sight,
it's what crossing eyes
sleep in when confused
and despised,
and older roads,
they represent
the small fortune's demise,
support the deterioration
of a misguided generation,
I scream,
"Generosity!"
I scream,
"Sincerity!"
I scream,
"Impoverished, oh,
it's all the same!"
But I rest
in my
holy-colloquialisms
of a required dosage
of one more rain.

I shook their palms
and kissed their feet
and washed their gardens
of raspberries and weeds,
I cut them
short of the grass wages,
I caught sight
of their futile engagements,
entertainment,
the corner-bar of
the robotic
and charged,
the parasite of anger
and tension,
I offered them the lactic pint
and sip, did they,
willingly.
When the wasp stings,
the wasp strikes again,
at the weakest,
the wasp learns from the bee
and dies in guilt.
In my orderly temptation,
do I hesitate, my
formation,
the societal stroke stroke-again,
aneurysm-rhythm to the dementia percussion,
the irony of the brass-men,
provoked to sing,
they are then frightened, blue.
They sing in groups,
a hive of aging,
still they change
the spirit of the time, but
if the time had lasted,

a mould they would have cast,
the duelling partition,
the cruel, false audition
of the rhyming heroes named
Calmly and Truthfully,
an oligarchy
of berries
where one caught the defined and true
mould,
influencing the other berries,
why I should have
buried the berries,
why I am the cloud,
I shall share only decay
on this graveyard world,
shrivelled, turned
against and over.
My mighty impact,
I am the crater upon your
doomed and extinguished history,
avoided, the centre,
below my deadly core,
knock once, I answer you
from behind the
door,
from loud hinges,
a forecast of the forgotten wishes,
my precipitation,
your anticipation,
your false pain,
the leaking tears of
one more rain.

Teachings of Continuity, Part Four: The Cake and The Latte

Heated glass
on deep French twine,
with my hair hanging like ribbons,
blackcurrant thrill to the seated spine.
Flaking chocolate of African origin,
I believed,
the shielded moisture, torn apart
by knife's unforgiving edge,
the cutlery sharper than any
practise-put dart.
Only for accuracy,
not for speed,
to compel me in my need,
propelling the fruit of divinity,
to the palette-washing dawn
of a European August.
Roasted, I stayed for midday,
the Sun resting on the reflection
of the pane.
Smallest joy, I am in marital feud with
longest joy,
because longevity never truly satisfies.
My divorce to be with smallest joy,
my beating circulation, one of marriage past,
the beat,
exchange to newer commitments.

I adore your charm,
you fulfil my Wednesday gloom,
the life's meaning, to make my exchange,
staying in the same corner coffee-place,
residing near fruition
but never fully realised,
I wouldn't have it any other way
than this;
the cake and the latte.

About the Author

Ciaran Perks is an English poet and writer of the 'Illusory Poems' and the 'Studies of Continuity' creative writing collections. Growing up and living in Plymouth, Devon, he has currently written two books, 'Peacocks' and 'Studies of Continuity'. He is set to release many more poetry collections, continuing the themes of dreams and other illusory ideas.

www.ingramcontent.com/pod-product-compliance
Lightning Source LLC
Chambersburg PA
CBHW020942090426
42736CB00010B/1228
* 9 7 8 1 7 8 9 6 3 2 1 8 7 *